Commentary by Jim Allen

ICHIRO MAGIC!

KODANSHA INTERNATIONAL Tokyo • New York • London

Distributed in the United States by Kodansha America, Inc.,
575 Lexington Avenue, New York, NY 10022,
and in the United Kingdom and continental Europe by
Kodansha Europe Ltd., 95 Aldwych, London WC2B 4JF.

Published by Kodansha America, Inc.

WEB SITE: www.thejapanpage.com

ISBN 4-7700-2871-7
First edition, 2001
01 02 03 04 05   10 9 8 7 6 5 4 3 2 1

CONTENTS

HOW THE WIZARD WEAVES HIS MAGIC

It's the ultimate American dream: Ichiro Suzuki, who grew up playing America's national pastime in Japan, giving it everything he had, comes to America and makes the big time in the biggest way possible.

The soft-spoken right fielder of the Seattle Mariners has brought new excitement to major league baseball with his speed, his sure catches, his strong, accurate throws, and his ability to hit nearly any pitch any-where. But the more you know about the man known simply as Ichiro, the less you're surprised by anything he accomplishes.

When the final results of the All-Star balloting were announced on July 2, 2001, and Ichiro led both leagues in the voting—a first for a major league rookie—this is what he said: "I did not expect or imagine that I would be a starter in the All-Star Game. This is my first year in the major leagues and the All-Star Game is in Seattle, so it means a lot to me. I have been here only three months, but the people appreciate my talent." That night, with the Mariners in Arlington for a series against the Texas Rangers, Ichiro, who was being rested, came off the bench in the seventh with Seattle trailing. He struck out his first time up against Pat Mahomes, himself a veteran of Japanese baseball. Then, with two out in the top of the ninth, Ichiro came to bat again. This time he whacked a two-run homer to tie the game. The Mariners went on to win, 9–7, in the tenth.

Even though it was just Ichiro's fourth homer of the season, the

(Photo: Robert Beck/Sports Illustrated)

(Photo: Peter Read Miller/Sports Illustrated)

Rangers' All-Star catcher Ivan "Pudge" Rodriguez was moved to say what more than a few people were thinking: "Right now, Ichiro is the best player in baseball. When they need a gapper, he hits a gapper. When they need a homer, he hits a homer. He's an all-around player."

If Ichiro was taken aback by his landslide All-Star selection, it was because, unlike knocking an outside pitch past the shortstop, the balloting was beyond his control. On the field, Ichiro is in complete command, playing with a measured intensity that makes a spectator think: "This is how the game should be played."

Ichiro's play demands explanation. No one should be able to do the things he does. He has a history of constantly amazing people with his numbers, but the statistics are just the shadow—not the essence—of his accomplishments. The essence is about playing the game the right way—the way he learned as a boy from his father. It is a quest he pursues to this day.

It is a quest that led him to the face-off with the massive southpaw Randy Johnson in the All-Star Game on July 10, 2001, at Seattle's much-heralded Safeco Field. Batting leadoff for the American League, Ichiro smashed the second pitch of the game to Todd Helton behind first base. Johnson raced to cover first, but Ichiro's speed beat him to the bag.

A hit.

Again.

Afterward, Ichiro put the event in its proper perspective.

On the field, Ichiro is in complete command, playing with a measured intensity that makes a spectator think: "This is how the game should be played."

"First of all, I'm very honored to face Randy in the All-Star Game, rather than the fact I got a base hit off him," Ichiro said through an interpreter. "Randy is a great pitcher and he was a Mariner and wore No. 51 before me. One of the things I always keep in mind is to wear this No. 51 with good dignity."

How many times has America heard a sports superstar say something like that?

Ichiro's respect for baseball and the players who have mastered it is deep-seated and sincere. His drive to learn the game took him to the pinnacle of individual success in his home country and has made him a hero in the country where he now swings his bat. But in Japan as in the United States, baseball is as much about a team as about an individual. Paradoxically, in Japan, that meant Ichiro rejecting the complacency and conformity that too often passes for teamwork.

When he was Japan's biggest star, more than one visiting major leaguer dismissed Ichiro's chances for survival, let alone success, in the majors. After all, Ichiro didn't look like a major league hitter. He wasn't a hulk. And he had an awkward-looking swing. Nothing new, these doubts. Ichiro's first manager in Japan didn't think Ichiro knew how to hit either. Especially when the 19-year-old Ichiro refused to adopt a more conventional batting style. (Ichiro had tried it, found it wanting.)

Labeled a rebellious kid, Ichiro just kept working at his game, seeking his own perfection. Because of his unflagging effort, Ichiro grew to know, instinctively, what he's capable of. This has given him the strength to brush aside, somewhat brashly, inappropriate instructions from managers, and to dare, more brashly, to make the leap to the major leagues.

His brilliant success has made him a modern-day samurai—with his concentration, self-control, and quiet intensity—on both sides of the Pacific. *Newsweek* magazine, swept up in the emotion five years ago, called him "the new face of Japan" in a lackluster era.

Even so, if Ichiro's face represents something new in Japan, his heart is pure tradition, one that holds dear the notion that effort makes the man and that pride in one's craft is not an option.

THE MAKING OF ICHIRO

The Ichiro explosion that shook Japan in 1994 caused people to wonder how a player could come out of nowhere and suddenly become the best in the country. He was called an overnight success and a batting genius. The implication was that Ichiro's talent, while real, was of the superhuman variety.

Not so. Ichiro's story is fully human.

Ichiro is the second son of Yoshie and Nobuyuki Suzuki from the town of Toyoyama, near the city of Nagoya in central Japan. Nobuyuki,

the owner of an electrical appliance repair shop, was mad about baseball and served as coach of the local Little League team. Ichiro describes, in a series of interviews with the Japanese journalist Narumi Komatsu, that his first memories are of age three when his father made him the gift of a baseball and a red leather baseball glove.

"It made me so happy," he said. "If I had any treasures, they were that ball and glove."

From the time he was in nursery school, baseball was already a constant in Ichiro's life. He remembers watching the games of Nagoya's professional team, his father's beloved Chunichi Dragons, and by the time he started elementary school, Ichiro knew the rules of the game. That was when he was installed as a fixture on his dad's team—registered under an assumed name with a falsified age. Officially, Little League required a boy to be at least in the third grade, but although Ichiro's small size was probably a giveaway, nobody said a word. Most likely because, underage as he was, Ichiro was already so good.

When Nobuyuki later advised his athletic son to join the soccer team because his school didn't have a baseball team, Ichiro begged off. He asked his dad to give him baseball lessons instead. Nobuyuki agreed under one condition: Ichiro had to put in the effort. From that point on, until Ichiro went to junior high four years later, Nobuyuki would leave his shop every afternoon, and father and son would go off to the local ballpark armed with gloves, a catcher's mitt, a bat, and a bag of seventy baseballs—all of which it was Ichiro's responsibility to carry.

There were quarrels. In the beginning Ichiro would sometimes want to skip practice, but Nobuyuki would not hear of it and just head for the park. The sight of his father going off to the park alone was too much for Ichiro to bear, and he would soon follow.

Sometimes a battle would brew over his father's not buying him a toy or an ice cream, or Ichiro's wanting to quit practice early to watch something on TV. Despite some chilly silences, the practice field was always the place where father and son came together. Their daily exertions held an unspoken allure that neither the stubborn father nor the stubborn son could walk away from.

Each afternoon, Ichiro would practice the mechanics of pitching, fielding, and hitting. Hitting posed the biggest challenge. Nobuyuki could pitch and Ichiro could retrieve the balls he was able to hit, but the problem was more basic—Ichiro's bat wasn't making a whole lot of contact.

Nobuyuki tried toss batting, where a batter swings at a ball lobbed to him from someone standing a few feet away. That helped. Ichiro began making more contact, but just hitting a ball tossed innocuously to him grew old fast. So Nobuyuki came up with an alternative.

"Life and death" toss batting. Instead of standing to the side, Nobuyuki stood a few yards directly in front of Ichiro, who was now forced to learn how to hit the ball where he wanted—in order to avoid striking his father. They started with rubber-coated balls, but by the time Ichiro was in the fifth grade—and by far the best player on the local Little League team—they had switched to hard balls, which might indeed have killed Nobuyuki if he were hit by one.

Ichiro credits much of his development as a player not only to his father's effort but also to his father's fresh, amateur outlook: Nobuyuki was

unfamiliar with—and unencumbered by—the orthodox forms that Japanese baseball seemed to exist for. Certainly, "life and death" toss batting was a teaching tool that no one with professional experience would have come up with.

"It was all about what I needed to learn. He really had to consider what was best rather than just teaching by the book. I wanted to throw hard, so he needed to think about how to accomplish that; I wanted to hit the ball far, so he needed think about the best way to practice for that." Nobuyuki also encouraged Ichiro to imitate different players he saw on TV, and thus was born the one-legged swinging stance Ichiro used until 2000, which had its origins in the form of Kazunori Shinozuka, one of Japan's best hitters in the early eighties.

If the father, by his daily investment in time, was a demanding teacher, the son proved to be a demanding pupil. He was never satisfied to go half speed. In fielding practice, he always wanted the hardest balls hit to him. In catching practice, he always threw as hard as he could. "More than junior high school, more than high school," Ichiro says, "those four years with my father engraved in me the sense you need for baseball, the sense of how to hit the ball, how to throw it, how to catch it."

What was missing from Ichiro's practice sessions in the park with his father was the chance to really hit. While Nobuyuki tried to

(Photo: Robert Beck/Sports Illustrated)

(Photo: Robert Beck/Sports Illustrated)

keep the toss batting interesting by varying the delivery, speed, and angle of the pitches—as Ichiro trained his body to respond to everything his dad could throw at him—it was clear they needed a little more technology than the park allowed for.

Soon father and son began to make nightly visits to a batting center, where Ichiro, now in the third grade, proceeded to hit his share of 60-mph pitches. Within two years, he was having his way with 75-mph deliveries and becoming something of a local legend.

When Ichiro started junior high school and joined the baseball team, he began to practice every day with his teammates. This marked the end of the daily one-on-one with his father at the park. Now, instead of coaching Ichiro in the afternoon, Nobuyuki would watch the Toyoyama

(Photo: Robert Beck/Sports Illustrated)   (Photo: Robert Beck/Sports Illustrated)

Junior High School team practice. When that was over, he and Ichiro would go off to the batting center.

There the familiar backbeat of Ichiro's line drives provided a sense of continuity, as did Ichiro's rapidly developing skills. But Nobuyuki did not stand passively aside when his son was in the batter's box. If Ichiro went after a ball out of the strike zone, Nobuyuki would let him know about it with a paternal tongue-lashing.

When Ichiro outgrew the 75-mph settings at the batting center, Nobuyuki arranged to have a pitching machine cranked up to hurl 80 miles per hour. Since no one else at the batting center could handle this speed, Ichiro would have to call ahead each day to have the machine ready for him.

By the time Ichiro finished junior high school, having pitched his

(Photo: John W. McDonough/Sports Illustrated)

school to a third-place finish in the national tournament, father and son wanted to turn up the heat at the batting center again. Impossible—the machine could not be set any faster. The only option left to the father-coach was to move the plate forward to cut down on Ichiro's reaction time. They didn't stop until they had shortened the distance by six feet.

Ichiro recalls practicing at the batting center once when the cleanup hitter for a regional high school powerhouse was also there. "I was watching him and didn't think he was spectacularly good. It got me thinking, 'Maybe I could be a pro baseball player.'"

The end of junior high school is a crossroads for every Japanese family, and for the Suzukis it was no different. The quality of a child's high school affects his or her chances of gaining admission to a top-level university, which is in turn the gateway to a high-profile career track. Ichiro was an excellent student with a shot at a good academic school, but his mind was set on baseball. His main concern was which of three high schools would be most likely to lead to a pro career.

He settled on Aichi Engineering University's Nagoya Electric High School (known as Aikodai Meiden). The school's manager, Go Nakamura, had sent eleven players to the pro ranks, and Ichiro was hoping to increase that number by at least one. Nakamura remembers how stunned he was when he first met Ichiro. Here was this much sought after baseball prodigy, but how could a kid this gangly possibly hit or throw the ball with any authority?

Attending Meiden meant that Ichiro would have to move away from home to live in the team's dormitory. Obviously this would be a break with the past, but Ichiro thought he was ready for new adventure. Any illusions about an ideal high school baseball life quickly vanished, however, when Nakamura told the freshmen recruits that their time at Meiden would be the most demanding experience of their entire lives. Nakamura was not to be disbelieved.

One of the more bothersome tasks was doing the laundry. Every evening after practice, underclassmen were handed the team's wash. Because washers and dryers were few and so much laundry had to be done, the task involved an inordinate amount of waiting in line. This got on Ichiro's nerves, particularly as it meant forfeiting time that could be spent working out. Putting off his chores until morning only meant waiting in line behind similarly minded teammates. Ichiro's solution was to get up every day at 3 A.M., when no one was using the machines. This regimen allowed him to practice all he wanted—at the expense of several hours of sleep each night for two years.

Was all this practice worth it? The seniors had priority at the indoor batting cage and in the gym. His recourse was to run laps on the track and swing his bat on the tennis courts. It may simply be that Ichiro had become so used to daily workouts that the thought of wasting time held a hidden terror for him.

Manager Nakamura noticed quickly that Ichiro was different from his teammates. "He was something else when it came to his power of concentration. Even in practice, he didn't take his time. He was the type who would quickly focus on the task and get it done."

No matter what his years of training had prepared him for on the diamond, he had not anticipated the harsh world of Japanese high school athletics. In addition to doing the laundry, first- and second-year players were required to endure arbitrary punishments at the hands of upper-classmen for the slightest misstep. Talking back to a senior, or being caught buying an ice cream, or doing a poor job cooking the rice meant being forced to kneel, balanced on the lid of a 1½-foot-tall steel garbage can, for a half hour. This was not pleasant, but with baseball at the center of his life, Ichiro did not let it bother him. He was where he wanted to be.

Koshien, the name of a stadium near Osaka, is the sun around which Japanese high school baseball revolves. When the two national high school baseball tournaments are held there each spring and summer, all Japan focuses on Koshien. The final game of the summer tournament is one of the major events on the nation's sports calendar.

As part of the Meiden team, Ichiro made the trip to Koshien twice. In his second year, when he was just another player, Meiden reached the finals of Koshien, having won the regional tournament, but lost in the first round. Meiden made it to the spring invitational tourna-ment the following year on the strength of its emerging superstar, one Ichiro Suzuki. But again, Ichiro's time on the national stage lasted for just one game.

Two first-round defeats would not keep the pro scouts away. In the regional qualifying tournament leading up to the next national summer

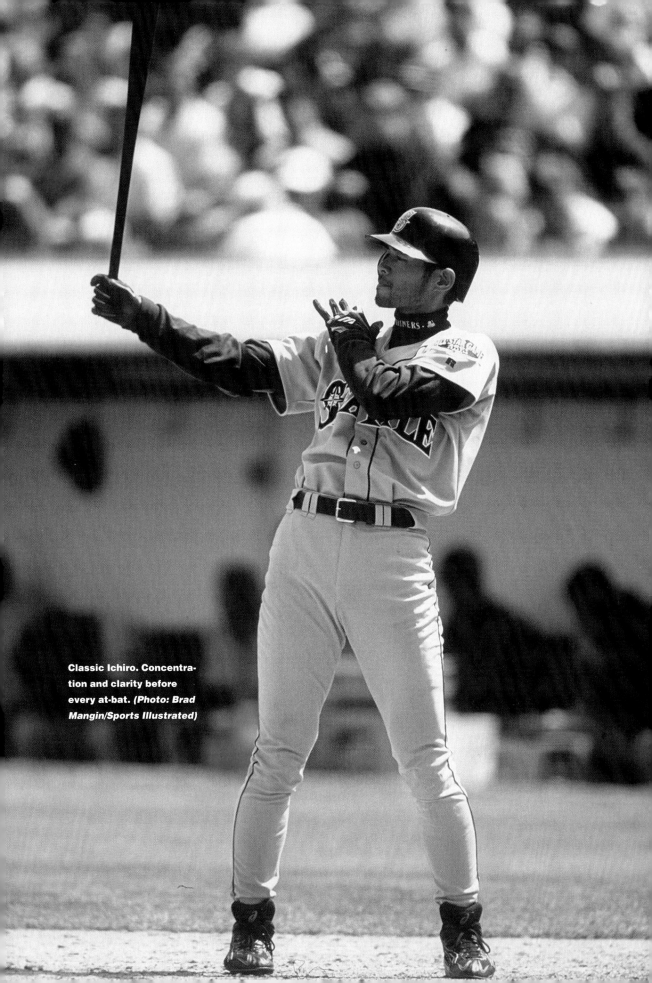

Classic Ichiro. Concentration and clarity before every at-bat. (Photo: Brad Mangin/Sports Illustrated)

Laying down a surprise bunt against Cleveland at Jacobs Field, August 3, 2001. Ichiro's hit advanced David Bell to third base, setting in motion a two-run rally in the eighth inning. The Mariners went on to win, 2–1. *(Photo: AFP/CORBIS)*

Below: Ichiro, in the dugout, awaits his next at-bat, in San Diego, June 17, 2001. *(Photo: V.J. Lovero/Sports Illustrated)*

Stretching, stretching, and more stretching, above, before the game in Denver, June 14, 2001. *(Photo: Reuters NewMedia Inc./CORBIS)* Below: In a game against the Yankees in Seattle, May 5, 2001, Ichiro makes a hard throw to third. That's Mariner center fielder Mike Cameron next to Ichiro and Yankee Jorge Posada in the foreground. *(Photo: Peter Read Miller/Sports Illustrated)*

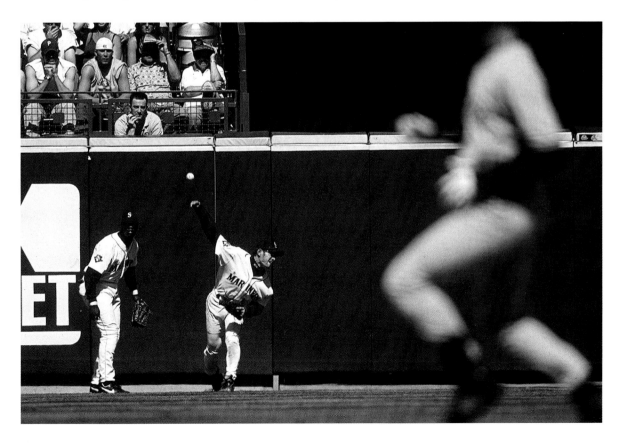

As Boston Red Sox pitcher Hideo Nomo hurls the ball, above, Ichiro looks for his chances down the third base line; May 8, 2001, at Fenway Park. *(Photo: AFP/CORBIS)* Right: Meeting the ball against the Angels at Edison International Field in Anaheim, June 30. 2001. *(Photo: V.J. Lovero/Sports Illustrated)*

Opposite: Anticipating the hit-by-pitch, July 7, 2001, at Dodger Stadium in Los Angeles. *(Photo: Robert Beck/Sports Illustrated)*

In a Seattle game against the Toronto Blue Jays, May 5, 2001, Ichiro heads for first. Catcher Darrin Fletcher is behind him. *(Photo: Peter Read Miller/Sports Illustrated)*

Sand and steal. *(Photo: © 2001 Don Smith/MLB Photos)*

At Dodger Stadium, July 7, 2001, tooling around the bases. *(Photo: Peter Read Miller/Sports Illustrated)*

At the All-Star Game in Seattle, July 10, 2001, Ichiro shares his exercise techniques with Yankee Derek Jeter, as Yankee first base coach, Lee Mazzili, looks on. *(Photo: © 2001 Rich Pilling/MLB Photos)*

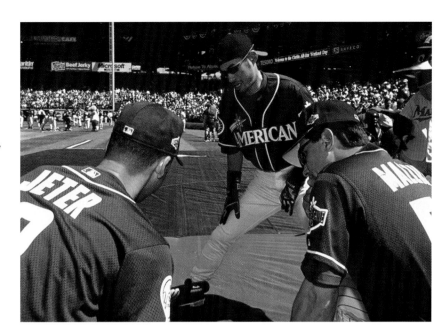

A true believer at Safeco Field as the Mariners take on the Anaheim Angels, April 20, 2001. Ichiro extended his hitting streak to 15 games. *(Photo: AFP/CORBIS)*

Ichiro and closer Kazuhiro Sasaki greet each other as the Mariners gather on the field to congratulate themselves after a 4–1 victory against Anaheim, April 20, 2001. Ichiro hit in his fifteenth straight game, Sasaki picked up his ninth save. The Mariners' victory lineup has been the most common post-game sight in the major leagues in the 2001 season. *(Photo: AFP/CORBIS)*

(Photo: Robert Beck/Sports Illustrated)

(Photo © 2001 John Williamson/MLB Photos)

championship, Ichiro powered Meiden to within a win of a third straight trip to Koshien. He hit .720 in the first eight qualifying games before going 0-for-3 in the final, which the team lost, 7–0.

Unlike his teammates, Ichiro was not crushed by missing a last chance at high school baseball glory. The team had done all it could do. Besides, Ichiro was looking ahead to the next challenge—making it as a pro.

(Photo: © 2001 Ron Vesely/MLB Photos)

(Photo: © 2001 Andy Hoyt/MLB Photos)

(Photo: © 2001 Brad Mangin/MLB Photos)

HEADING TO KOBE

Ichiro could hit, of course, but he had long expected to be a pitcher. His dreams of a mound career were run off the road, literally, when a passing car knocked him off his bicycle in his second year at Meiden. After a month on crutches, he returned to the team and played first base until he healed completely. By the time he returned to the mound a few months later, he'd picked up some bad throwing habits from his stint at first. The chances of his developing into a pitcher who could take a scout's breath away had dimmed.

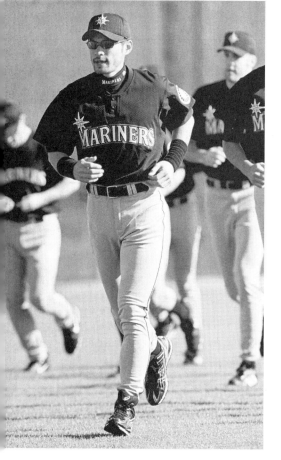

Warming up at winter training camp in Peoria, Arizona. (Photo: Reuters NewMedia Inc./CORBIS)

But Ichiro's ability to hit was never in doubt, and when time for the pro draft came, scouts had little trouble finding a spot for him somewhere on the field. Ichiro was selected in the fourth round by the Kobe-based Orix BlueWave.

Nobuyuki was disappointed that his son was not picked earlier in the draft and had not gone to their favorite team, the Chunichi Dragons. Ichiro was unfazed.

Although it was just a short trip by train from the high school baseball mecca of Koshien, Ichiro had never been to Kobe, a cosmopolitan port city west of Osaka. For him, as with many Japanese baseball fans, the name BlueWave conjured up little more than a blank. That too was of little concern to Ichiro. He was going to be a pro ballplayer! That mattered.

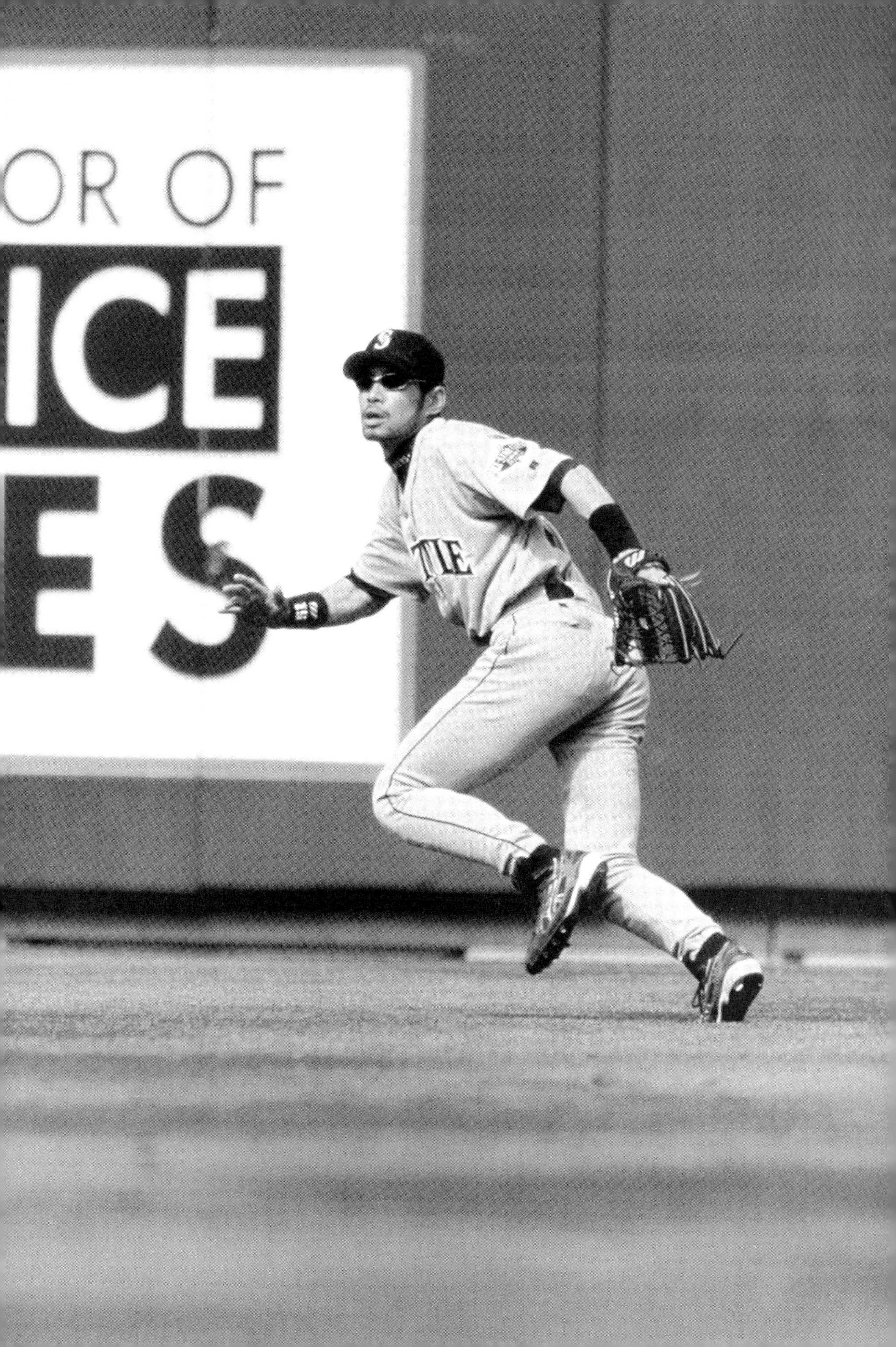
OR OF
ICE
ES

(Photo: © 2001 Brad Mangin/MLB Photos)   (Photo: Robert Beck/Sports Illustrated)

When Ichiro got to the Orix organization, he looked around and sized up the situation. A lot of the guys trying to make the team were slow, far from great. Ichiro figured his time on the farm team would be brief.

Yet, when he got the call to join the big club in July, the man who his Mariners' teammates now call the "Wizard" was still a sorcerer's apprentice. He found himself hesitant to go. To be Ichiro means to know when you're ready, and Ichiro wasn't sure he could handle pro-level pitching the way he wanted to. He went anyway, yo-yo-ing between the Pacific League, one of Japan's two big leagues, and the Western League, which Orix's farm team played in. While the pitching was better in the PL, Ichiro managed to hit well enough (a .253 batting average in 40 games as a reserve) to raise his hopes of making the roster of the big club the following year.

(Photo: Brad Mangin/Sports Illustrated)   (Photo: Robert Beck/Sports Illustrated)

The golden moment of his first pro season came when he was named the MVP of the minor league All-Star Game. His first time up, Ichiro had planned to knock the ball through the left side of the infield, but a look to his father in the stands changed his mind. His dad signaled him to pull the ball to the right. Ichiro did exactly that—lining it over the fence. He later added a single and stole second and third.

"I like to steal. I'm good at it," Ichiro told an interviewer for Japan's *Baseball Magazine* after the game. "When I steal third, unlike when it's really close at second, I want to cruise in . . . without sliding, so I can really surprise people."

The 18-year-old rookie admitted that his goal was winning a batting title and leading the league in stolen bases. In retrospect, one wonders why Ichiro mentioned no goal of receiving an MVP award or two, but

then again such things depend on the goodwill of others. He could only depend on himself. And indeed, by the time he left for the majors, Ichiro had racked up seven straight PL batting titles and one stolen-base crown.

Ichiro ended that first year with a .366 average, winning the Western League batting championship by a wide margin. It must have meant something to the young player, but it meant little within the organization.

Ichiro started the first two games of 1993 but didn't hit well. He soon found himself back in the Western League. He was promoted and demoted three times that season, all while he continued to demolish minor league pitching—hitting for an even better average with more power and more walks.

His third PL start of the season came on June 12, the BlueWave facing Hideo Nomo, a pitcher who, now well known to American fans, was a year away from the arm troubles that endangered his career. Here was a chance for Ichiro to show what he could do against the best pitcher in the league. His first time up, he singled to right. Next time up, he fouled out. He fouled out again. Then, with the Orix trying to rally from a five-run deficit, he took Nomo deep.

The home run made Ichiro a marked man, but in a way few would have predicted. Rather than congratulations, he received a lecture from the Orix coaching staff about his proper place in the baseball world, which would be on the farm team unless he (1) stopped trying to hit home runs and (2) gave up his unorthodox hitting style and followed the instructions of the batting coach.

Willingness to conform is a sign of good manners in Japan—a

sign that you accept your place within the group you belong to. Those unwilling to play by the rules get punished. Ichiro had tried to do as the batting coach instructed. He did it all through the first off-season with the BlueWave and kept at it until spring, stopping only when he saw clearly that it wasn't working. But in Japanese ball, he wasn't supposed to think for himself.

Even with minor league demotion in the balance, Ichiro refused to give in. "I was thinking, 'What if there was a different coach every year? I'd have to change my style to suit each one of them.' I wouldn't be playing very long if I did that. Some people always have the most fashionable clothes or brand-name things, but they may not have their own style. It's

the same thing with baseball. If I changed myself to make the coaches happy, in the end you wouldn't know what kind of player I am. My personal style would be destroyed."

The coach even tried to get Nobuyuki to intervene. Not surprisingly, dad said it would be of no use. Ichiro had never been one to change his course once he'd decided on it.

If Ichiro's being with the big club meant being in the doghouse, the farm team was an oasis. Orix's minor league batting coach, Kenichiro Kawamura, earned the respect of both Suzukis with his sensible approach to Ichiro's batting style. They credit Kawamura with adding the final touches to Ichiro's technique in the batter's box.

Tossing the ball to fans at the All-Star Game—
a personal tradition Ichiro began with fans in Japan.

"Kawamura quickly recognized my peculiar characteristics as a hitter and was always willing to work with me," Ichiro said. "Demotion to the farm team was fine because Kawamura was there."

Rather than trying to knock down what Ichiro had built up over years of effort—and it was obviously something that worked—Kawamura gave Ichiro a way to go beyond what he was already doing. Starting with videos of Ichiro swinging in high school, the coach worked on timing: how to determine the path of the ball and how to find the point of contact. The result of their collaboration was what became Ichiro's trademark pendulum leg-swing. Ichiro hammered out the kinks during fall camp and kept working on it in November.

The venue was Hawaii, where Ichiro and several Orix teammates were sent for the Hawaiian Winter League. Playing for the Hilo Stars on the Big Island, Ichiro hit with ease. And despite the press mistakenly reporting his name as "Ichido"—which in Japanese means "once" or "for one time"—it was becoming evident to all that this Suzuki was no one-time success.

"The way he hit in the minors for two straight years was incredible," said BlueWave outfielder So Taguchi, who was in Hilo with Ichiro. "And then in Hawaii, he showed he could hit as well as those big hitters who weren't from Japan. I guess, when he won his first batting title the next year, I wasn't really surprised."

In Hawaii, Ichiro met Akira Ogi, the Orix's new manager. Ogi had managed Nomo at the Kintetsu Buffaloes for three years and had been happy to let Nomo pitch his heart out without forcing him to change

Mark McLemore and Ichiro do their version of a high five as they come home on Edgar Martinez's two-run RBI against the Athletics; in Oakland, June 21, 2001. *(Photo: AFP/CORBIS)*

(Photo: Reuters NewMedia Inc./CORBIS)

(Photo: Brad Mangin/Sports Illustrate

his unorthodox tornado-style wind-up. Ogi's approach with Ichiro was much the same: Do what works.

When he first laid eyes on Ogi, the usually unflappable Ichiro was at a loss. His new manager looked for all the world like a yakuza, a Japanese gangster—dressed in white slacks, white belt, and white shoes, and wearing gold-framed sunglasses.

But Ogi and Ichiro had a lot in common. They were both perfectionists who wanted to win in the worst way—Ogi never had a losing season until 2000—and the changes that Ogi brought to the team saw instant results. With Ogi, if you hustled, you played, which meant that everyone would get a chance to show his stuff. Ichiro went to Ogi and said he wanted to play; he never stopped hustling, never stopped practicing, and he was the only member of the team to play in every one of Orix's 130 games in 1994.

Unlike the previous regime's batting coach, the coach brought in by Ogi counseled Ichiro to just go out and hit. It was music to the ears of the hip-hop–loving hitting machine, whose first name would soon be the best known in Japan.

Ogi must have known the kid had something special. One indication of this was that prior to spring training, Ogi instituted another change. Instead of the name "Suzuki" on the back of No. 51's jersey, the new skipper wanted the name to read "Ichiro."

Below: Mariners beat the Blue Jays; McLemore bows to Ichiro; at Toronto, May 12, 2001.

(Photo: Reuters NewMedia Inc./CORBIS)

Overleaf: At the All-Star Game, Arizona's Randy Johnson, who once wore No. 51 for Seattle, tries to pick off Seattle's current No. 51. *(Photo: V.J. Lovero/Sports Illustrated)*

ICHIRO-MANIA

It was a terrific season for the Orix in 1994. Ichiro had a pair of 23-game hitting streaks and became an overnight star. His batting average hovered just below .400 all season.

A light moment with the New York Mets mascot during American League practice for the All-Star Game. (Photo: Reuters NewMedia Inc./CORBIS)

Ichiro-mania struck Japan with the force of a typhoon, and it couldn't have happened at a better time for the lords of Japanese baseball. Professional soccer had recently made its debut in Japan, and the rush of popularity that sport immediately enjoyed was a wake-up call to the baseball establishment. Indeed, baseball and its players had come to be seen by many as the epitome of Japan's complacent corporate society.

But Ichiro was a new breed in many ways, someone who had rejected conformity when it hindered results. As his star rose, his popularity surged. It was something to behold. People turned up everywhere the BlueWave played—just to get a glimpse of the country's newest sensation. When Ichiro completed his last at-bat of the night, masses of fans would leave for the exits.

In the early stages of the 1994 season, Ichiro found he had an enormous advantage over the pitchers he faced: They knew only of his unimpressive Pacific League statistics. With only six teams in each of Japan's top leagues, the collection and analysis of mountains of data on every opposition player are routine. This attention to detail is considered an integral part of the game by Japanese baseball insiders. But because no

Surrounded by Bernie Williams of the Yankees, who also wears No. 51, and Kazu Sasaki and his children at the All-Star Game festivities.
(Photo: © 2001 Rich Pilling/MLB Photos)

San Francisco's Barry Bonds, the National League top vote getter, and Ichiro, the American League's top vote getter. Ichiro also holds the trophy for the most votes received in both leagues.
(Photo: © 2001 Allen Kee/MLB Photos)

Harold Reynolds, a former Mariners All-Star himself, introduces Ichiro to the fans.
(Photo: © 2001 Rich Pilling/MLB Photos)

one considers a player's minor league performance to be significant, teams paid little heed to the skinny outfielder. There were, they thought, more dangerous hitters in the lineup.

Ichiro's career batting average in the PL was a puny .226, with almost no power and no walks. So pitchers challenged him. Ichiro made them pay. He had 4 of his 13 home runs in the first 17 games. Word began to spread: The kid was dangerous. Fans were knocked out, jazzed by the prospect of this young unknown hitting .400 or breaking the 200-hit barrier for the first time ever in Japan's short season (the record was 191 in 140 games).

Ichiro's ability to concentrate had always allowed him to shut out the distractions and to focus on what he wanted to accomplish. But as his popularity grew with each hit, things began to change. Starting the season with the simple resolution to perform his best for the 130 games, Ichiro became painfully aware that as much as his team needed him, he was also carrying the aspirations of a whole nation.

But instead of struggling under the weight of such expectations, Ichiro thrived. He produced, and he produced. No news or sports broadcast was complete without an Ichiro update showing videotape of every single plate appearance and reporting on his batting average. The Ichiro watch continued for several seasons and has been revived—in a big way—with his extraordinary season with the Seattle Mariners as they have torn up the major leagues.

The BlueWave peaked that 1994 breakthrough year when they reached first place on August 16. Ironically, it was a day when Ichiro went 0-for-3 and his second 23-game streak of the season ground to a halt. The team's pennant hopes drifted out to sea after it was swept in a four-game series that ended on September 19. But the next day, Ichiro broke the 200-hit barrier by going 4-for-5.

In an effort to push the record as far as he could, Ichiro started to swing at every pitch he could reach and, uncharacteristically, began to strike out a lot, with 10 of his 53 whiffs coming in the last eight games of the year. He managed to bring his total to 210 hits—19 more than the previous record.

At a school in the Seattle area early into the season, Ichiro told the students who aspired to be baseball players that taking care of their equipment, even if they were sticks used in place of bats, was a prerequisite for learning the game.

Becoming an on-field wizard had deprived Ichiro of his power to disappear. He was no longer able to walk the streets by himself without being mobbed. Thus it was a great relief when an off-season commercial resulted in his receiving a free car. He'd been riding to the ballpark with teammate Taguchi all season. With his own wheels, he was now afforded the luxury of some privacy. Of course, meticulous as Ichiro has always been about important things in his life, he washed and maintained the car with the same careful attention that he paid to his batting style. Other players would allow beat reporters, hoping for some parting words after a

The lineup for the 2001 American League All-Star team: from left, manager Joe Torre of the Yan-kees, Ichiro, A-Rod of Texas, Manny Ramirez of the Red Sox, the Mariners' Bret Boone, Juan Gon-zales of Cleveland, and the Mariners' John Olerud. With Edgar Martinez, just out of the picture, and Mike Cameron, Kazu Sasaki, and Jeff Nelson, there were eight Mariners named to the All-Star team. *(Photo: @ 2001 Rich Pilling/MLB Photos)*

game, to crowd around their cars. Not Ichiro. He asked the press to keep their distance. It is a testament to the regard people had for him that, for the most part, they did.

Although famous for his unorthodox style and sense of individuality, Ichiro was never a rebel. He adopted wholeheartedly the Japanese game's fondness for small details and the principle that baseball was a craft to be mastered. He echoed the Japanese baseball mantra that because of their physical limitations, Japanese players can only compete with larger non-Japanese players through greater devotion and attention to the fine points.

Upon joining the Mariners, he cringed to see his teammates tossing their gloves roughly into their lockers. He had been taught to respect the tools of the game. At a school in the Seattle area early into the season, Ichiro told the students who aspired to be baseball players that taking care of their equipment, even if they were sticks used in place of bats, was a prerequisite for learning the game.

JUST CAN'T GET NO SATISFACTION

As Ichiro ended the 1994 season batting .385, attendance at Orix games—at home and on the road—had improved by four thousand fans per game.

He was named the Pacific League's MVP—an unusual honor for a player on a second-place team. Ichiro was a more conventional MVP selection in each of the next two seasons as he led the BlueWave to consecutive league titles. But generating the level of satisfaction of his breakthrough season proved a harder task than winning a pennant.

On January 17, 1995, the city of Kobe, home to the BlueWave, was shaken by a colossal earthquake that left more than 5,000 people dead. Ichiro was in the team dormitory when the tremors struck, but he sustained no injury. Even so, the trauma of the earthquake left him unnerved, and he packed up and left to resume his off-season training at his home near Nagoya. This would not seem untoward, but because of who he was, there was talk that he had deserted the city in its time of need, and this cut deeply.

Despite the city's devastation, attendance at BlueWave games grew in 1995, as Kobe began the tough process of rebuilding itself. The club responded by overachieving in what was to be a banner year.

As the end of the season neared, with only one game to clinch the pennant, the BlueWave proceeded to lose its last four games at home. But on the road they came through with a resounding victory. Of course, the championship brought joy to Kobe, but it was a pleasure diminished by the begrudging sense that, as a team, the players had let the city down. They had failed to win the pennant at home, and in the aftermath of the earthquake, they'd cheated their fans of the thrill of victory. The sentiment was only reinforced when the overmatched BlueWave were rousted out of the Japan Series in five games.

"I think there are different kinds of championships, the ones you seize and the ones you win because another club chokes," Ichiro said, viewing the season philosophically. "The 1995 pennant lacked a sense of achievement. We were lucky."

Overleaf: Safeco Field, home of the Seattle Mariners. Under construction for over two years, Safeco opened in July 1999 with an official capacity of 46,621. The stadium boasts, in addition to views of the Seattle skyline and Puget Sound, real grass, a retractable roof, trains running under the east roof trestle, and earthquake protection, which withstood the 6.8-magnitude tremors that shook Seattle on February 28, 2001. *(Photo: © 2001 Ben Van Houten/MLB Photos)*

Drilled in the back by a pitch by Hideo Nomo; at Safeco against Boston, May 2, 2001. It was
Ichiro's first hit-by-pitch in the major leagues. The Mariners went on to win, 5–1.
(Photo: Reuters NewMedia Inc./CORBIS)

Orix won the pennant again in 1996, and then went on to win the Japan Series when the Yomiuri Giants, the country's most popular team botched it. For Ichiro, however, the victory was tainted. "A really strong team goes out from the start of the season and puts a stranglehold on the title. We only started to play hard when it was clear that we had a chance to win in the second half of the season. We weren't a strong team."

The guy wins a championship, and he's not happy. But he did not grumble when, that same year, he was stopped two games shy of equaling his year-old record of reaching base in 69 consecutive games.

The streak ended after an epic confrontation with a hard throwing right-hander by the name of Hideki Irabu—in Ichiro's opinion, the best pitcher in Japan at the time. Ichiro faced Irabu three times that night, and twice he struck out. "The pitches Irabu threw in that game were really something. I was satisfied with the outcome even though I struck out. If you say 'How can you be satisfied?' it's because it was pure strength against strength. Between us there was a child-like feeling. I had to get a hit—just because it was him—and he couldn't allow a hit—just because it was me. Neither one of us would budge. I've never spoken to him about it directly, but that was the very vivid sense I had. The fans felt it too and enjoyed it more because of it."

After his first big season, when Ichiro experienced the personal triumph of establishing himself as a pro, this kind of man-to-man battle, which Ichiro longed for, became rarer by the day. The opposition began a strategy of avoiding him at all costs. In 1995, he was hit by pitches 18 times and walked intentionally 17 times, beginning a run of six straight seasons as the league leader in the latter category.

The pure combat that Japanese baseball espouses had been sub-
verted by the controlled, micro-managed style that now dominates the
game. Here was the paradox all over again: In a country where the war-
rior's code of honor was the ideal—even if it was something closer to fan-
tasy than history—conformity, complacency, and the easy way out had
become the way to succeed.

Things began to gnaw at Ichiro's spirit.

MAJOR LEAGUE ATTITUDE

In retrospect, the highlight of 1996 came after the season ended, with the
biannual series between Japan's top pros and touring major league all-
stars from the United States. The series resumed after a four-year hiatus—
the 1994 tour having been canceled because of the players' strike. On the
Japanese side, Ichiro was the marquee player.

In the first game at Tokyo Dome, Ichiro squared off against
Hideo Nomo, who had become a star with the Los Angeles Dodgers, in a
truly electric moment. With so many camera flashes going off, the stadium
lighting seemed almost superfluous. The battle with Nomo, however, was
only a small part of the story, as was Ichiro's 7-for-11 batting performance.
Joining Nomo were Cal Ripken Jr., Mike Piazza, Barry Bonds, and a pair
of Seattle Mariners—Ken Griffey Jr. and Alex Rodriguez.

Ichiro's first contact with these major league all-stars made a pro-
found impact on him. Despite their daunting form, the pitchers did not
awe Ichiro with their speed. What impressed him more were the hitters—
in particular, their ability to take charge in the batter's box regardless of

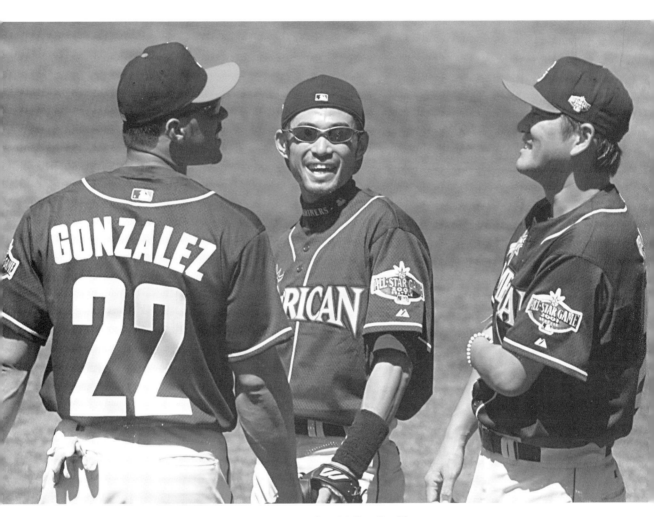

At the All-Star Game, with Cleveland's Juan Gonzales and Seattle's Kazu Sasaki.

(Photo: AFP/CORBIS)

what the pitcher threw them. They were able to hold back on curves, swinging no less powerfully than they did at fastballs. In each at-bat, they imposed their will on the game.

Ichiro told Rodriguez that it would be a privilege for him to play alongside these great players, but one gets the impression that, deep down, Ichiro felt pretty confident that he would fit right in.

When Ichiro told team officials of his desire to play in the majors, they laughed—despite the fact that they were in the process of selling pitcher Shigetoshi Hasegawa's contract to the Anaheim Angels.

Hasegawa had never made a secret of his desire to live and play in the United States. The Orix had politely rejected his pleas until he had the first poor year of his career. Suddenly, the right-hander was expendable. But Ichiro, a 23-year-old, three-time MVP, was another case altogether.

When the 1997 season started, Ichiro's game began to lose its edge as he entered a two-year period of struggle with his form. Asked if the pressure to add a fourth straight batting crown to his trophy case was beginning to weigh on his shoulders, Ichiro answered that that was never the issue. "Winning is the most important thing. But the players were not gearing up for a third straight title. It was pretty lame. You can't have that kind of thing, especially after our experiences in 1995 and 1996. In that atmosphere, a batter has to work to get results since raising your spirits and maintaining your motivation is definitely difficult. Because I was able to put up decent numbers, I could maintain my motivation that way. That was where my pursuit of consecutive batting titles came from."

Ichiro was good enough to win two more batting titles, in 1997 and 1998, but his status as the best player in the country was no longer supported by his performance. Ichiro had run into a wall—and knowing something was wrong forced him to put his major league ambition on hold.

He played well when the next group of major league all-stars visited in 1998, but he didn't stand head and shoulders above the competition the way he had two years earlier. Mike Hargrove, then manager of the Cleveland Indians, who skippered the 1998 tour, was asked at the time what he thought of Japan's rising sons. His response: Ichiro could play on any major league team—as a fourth or fifth outfielder.

Even in the darkest times, Ichiro could transform a ball game like few others. He remained a crowd pleaser who absorbed the fans' energy and radiated it back, brightening up the entire ballpark experience. Before the game, he would catch fungoes behind his back. Even throwing the ball around in the outfield became part of the show. When warming up in right field, he would throw, not to center, but all the way across the outfield, from foul pole to foul pole, to the left fielder, drawing the kind of response usually reserved for displays of fireworks.

On occasion, when manager Ogi would embark on long-winded arguments with the umpire, the child in Ichiro would get the better of him. During one particularly long Ogi monologue in Tokyo, as other fielders tossed the ball around, Ichiro started playing catch with the home team's fans in the right-field seats. Another time, Ichiro, the once-pitcher, snuck onto the mound with a smile that his face could barely contain and began to throw the ball to the catcher as the crowd roared its approval.

In the 1996 mid-season All-Star series, Ogi was a co-conspirator as he brought Ichiro in from right field to pitch to the Central League's top slugger, Hideki Matsui. But the CL manager, one of the grumpier old men of the game, pulled the plug on the fun by sending a relief pitcher in to pinch-hit against Ichiro.

But even in the carnival atmosphere of the All-Star games, a streak of six straight losses by the once-dominant PL All-Stars caused Ichiro to question his teammates' motivation.

Mike Hargrove, then manager of the Cleveland Indians, who skippered the 1998 tour, was asked at the time what he thought of Japan's rising sons. His response: Ichiro could play on any major league team— as a fourth or fifth outfielder.

NEW MAN

As the 1999 season approached, it appeared that Ichiro was going nowhere fast, but a series of events occurred in quick succession to restore his faith.

As part of their working agreement with the Seattle Mariners, the BlueWave sent Ichiro along with a handful of players to the Mariners'

In the dugout with catcher Tom Lampkin and manager Lou Piniella.

(Photo: Brad Mangin/Sports Illustrated)

(Photo: Robert Beck/Sports Illustrated)

camp at Peoria, Arizona. There, Ichiro renewed his acquaintance with Griffey and A-Rod and began to get a better feel for life in the major leagues, even though a bad spare-rib dinner incapacitated him for all but a couple of games.

A queasy stomach, the slow pace of camp, and the number of out-of-shape players he saw did little to lessen Ichiro's appetite for a season-long diet of major league pitching. He was not due to become a free agent until after the 2001 season, but what was of greater concern was the fact that, since the 1994 season, he had lacked deep confidence in his hitting. That was about to change.

Understanding what was wrong had eluded him despite the incredible number of hours he logged in the batting cage month after month and year after year. After starting the 1999 season by going 7-for-31, he suddenly discovered that the angle of his front foot was off slightly, disrupting his timing and resulting in easy outs on balls he should have hit squarely.

Once that revelation came, Ichiro again felt in charge of his destiny. For two seasons, he went on a rampage. He finished the 1999 season with a career-best .572 slugging percentage. In 2000, he again flirted with .400 before settling for a career-best .387 batting average and, with it, a seventh-straight batting championship.

Good enough, but like a master swordsman in a samurai drama, Ichiro had begun to handicap himself. With a future in the majors in mind, he wanted to adjust his eye to the major league strike zone, which extends nearly to the edge of the batter's box on the other side of the plate. So when an at-bat didn't matter, Ichiro would go after pitches way off the plate.

In the summer of 1999, he again asked for permission to leave for the majors. Again, he was refused. Other players had gone without their club's permission, and it was conceivable that Ichiro could find a loophole, but that was not his way. He let the issue rest—not because of the organization's stance, but because Ogi asked him to.

Ichiro owed Ogi a debt of gratitude, and regardless of Ichiro's personal taste for hip clothes and hip-hop music, he was still an old-fashioned Japanese man, respectful to those who had helped him. Ogi had opened the door, giving him space to breathe, so it would have been unthinkable for Ichiro to ignore his manager's wishes.

During his time at the Mariners' camp, Seattle pitcher Mac Suzuki asked Ichiro if he'd be interested in talking with Mac's agent, Don Nomura. Ichiro demurred. He would have nothing to do with Nomura, a former pro himself who had found the loophole that freed Nomo to pitch in the majors. For that, Nomura was considered a traitor by the Japanese baseball establishment, and Ichiro reportedly told Mac he didn't want to deal with such a "bad man."

After the 1999 season ended, Ichiro embarked on a new phase of life. Giving up his bachelorhood, he married Yumiko Fukushima, a television and radio personality. The wedding took place in Los Angeles. All preparations were made in secret, the couple even taking separate flights to the States to avoid detection by the media. In addition to their families, Ichiro invited three or four friends, none of whom had any connection with baseball.

Resigned to staying in Japan until he became a free agent, Ichiro burned up the league until the middle of August 2000, when a muscle inflammation in the area of his rib cage ended his season. It was not long after this diagnosis that manager Ogi invited Ichiro and Yumiko to dinner. In the middle of the meal, Ogi casually mentioned, "I guess it would be all right for you to give it a shot." He was talking about the major leagues! Both Ichiro and his wife were floored.

With Ogi's permission, the team soon relented, but Ichiro's father was in no hurry to see him go. Nobuyuki wanted Ichiro to wait a year, but Ichiro, coming off the worst injury of his career, was in no mood to wait. A pro career could be cut short at any time, and Ichiro was not going to let this opportunity slip.

Nobuyuki finally relented, telling his son: "Life comes but once. Be bold. Go for it."

"WHASSUP, DOG?"

When the news was announced that Japan's biggest star was leaving, Nobuyuki's sentiment was echoed on a national scale. Despite Japan's many economic successes, the country still harbors a massive inferiority complex. The prospect of a Japanese position player becoming a successful major leaguer was tantalizing, but the excitement was tempered by fear that he might fail.

But Ichiro knew what he was doing. Asked if he was nervous upon reaching an agreement with the Mariners, Ichiro replied that if he didn't think he could cut it, he wouldn't be signing with them in the first place.

(Photo: Robert Beck/Sports Illustrated)

Conferring with coach John McLaren, left, and manager Lou Piniella. *(Photo: Robert Beck/Sports Illustrated)*

Half of the thirty major league teams put in a bid for Ichiro's negotiating rights. The Mariners' winning bid of $13,125,000 raised more than a few eyebrows on both sides of the Pacific. A major league all-star team happened to be touring Japan at the time, and some players expressed the feeling that that was a lot of money just to talk to an unproven player.

The Mariners, according to Bob Finnigan of the *Seattle Times*, realistically expected Ichiro to hit .270 to .280 in his first major league season. Someone who might make a lead-off hitter.

Ichiro's first exhibition hit was a bouncer up the middle that the pitcher nearly snared. It made front-page news everywhere in Japan. But the number of balls Ichiro did not hit solidly made it appear that Ichiro was not the hitter the Mariners had in mind. Thus it made sense that manager Lou Piniella should tell Ichiro to drive the ball to right.

The surprise came when the rookie refused, wrote Art Thiel in the *Seattle Post-Intelligencer*. "I'm just setting them up," Ichiro is reported to have said, "them" meaning the pitchers. "No problem."

Al Martin, Ichiro's fellow Mariners outfielder, overheard the exchange and was incredulous. "Come on. Nobody is that good," he said to *Baseball Weekly*. "I'm sorry, it doesn't work that way." Martin is delighted to have been proven wrong, but what he was thinking isn't a whole lot different from what people in Japan were saying about the guy in 1994.

Being Ichiro means to be able to match your own expectations, which are always higher than anyone else's. Even so, Ichiro did manage to surprise himself on opening day, when his bunt single led to a big run in the Mariners' victory. Naturally, the Mariners had expected that Ichiro, coming from a country where the sacrifice bunt is considered a sacred act, would be super at it. You can imagine their astonishment when Ichiro revealed that he hadn't been asked to bunt in seven years.

Whether he doubted he could get the bunt down or not is something different entirely.

"I'm just setting them up," Ichiro is reported to have said, "them" meaning the pitchers. "No problem."

Just as he causes double takes with his habitual greeting to teammates of "Whassup, dog?" Ichiro has caused even more heads to shake with his defensive artistry.

"If I'm going to surprise American fans, it's going to be with my fielding and my arm," Ichiro said in his interviews with Komatsu. "If you are used to watching slow-footed fielders with poor fundamentals, then when you see someone who can move a little bit it must look good . . . I get a lot of joy out of the cheers behind me from the right-field stands. I'm curious how much excitement watching my play will generate."

The answer so far is, quite a bit.

It's now legend: In a game early in the season against the Oakland Athletics, Ichiro charged a single to right, got the ball off in a heartbeat, and unleashed a rifle shot to third base that nailed Terrence Long by three feet. Long walked off the field wondering where the ball came from.

(Overleaf photo: Robert Beck/Sports Illustrated)

Ichiro even scores when he doesn't. In a game against the Baltimore Orioles, Ichiro materialized out of nowhere to get to a foul fly, but at the last moment was robbed on the play by a fan. It was something so self-evident that the umpires called the batter out on fan interference. Orioles manager Mike Hargrove, whose assessment of Ichiro's talent has been upgraded since 1998, argued the call so much that the ump ejected him from the game.

Of course Ichiro reported that he had the ball all the way.

So right field is now known as Area 51, a reference not only to the number Ichiro wears but also to the site near Groom Lake, Nevada, where the unexpected has been known to occur.

ICHI-RRIFIC!

The Mariners made an extra effort to get Ichiro to Seattle, and they have worked overtime to make their newest player feel at home. Perhaps only Ichiro was prepared for the wave of popularity that has followed him across the Pacific, but it's unlikely that Ichiro was prepared for the wave of pure excitement that his presence has helped the Mariners to generate at every park they sail into.

It's not just the electronic billboard at Safeco Field or the crush of fans—if you think they're Japanese alone, look again—brandishing their Ichiro banners and dancing in the bleachers. In a sport where many a player is touted as a phenomenon, Ichiro is the genuine article. He makes the hype seem understated. It is his distinctiveness that we respond to, not his being Japanese—major league baseball is far too cosmopolitan, on the field at least, for that. The distinctiveness is, simply, his compelling command of the game's details.

Fact is, he's a bit retro, a throwback to the deadball era, when runs were scarce and speed and guile were often decisive. "Scientific baseball," as it was called at the time by John McGraw and Ty Cobb, was the art of the hit-and-run, the sacrifice, and the steal. In more recent times, this has been largely overshadowed by the might-makes-right of the long ball. Everybody loves a home run, but in today's game, small parks and mile-high altitudes have made home runs as common as bobble-head dolls. Where the big stars are the biggest boppers, Ichiro has reached out to our yearning for something more artistic, more beautiful to behold, than just another going-going-gone.

While Ichiro is as unique in the majors as he was in Japan, his style is a direct descendant of Ty Cobb's. Nearly a century ago, Japan took scientific baseball to be gospel and has since tried to maintain the standards of the pre–Babe Ruth game. At its best, the Japanese approach to baseball teaches that only discipline and attention to detail can make for success. Ichiro has echoed this sentiment, saying that the physically stronger major leaguers would be even better if they treated the game with the same, rather old-fashioned respect.

The thinking is stale, and the time capsule that is Ichiro's style is another example that little is ever really new, but there's no denying that Ichiro is fresh air to American baseball. He is a complete player, a man who knows his worth yet knows the meaning of the word *humility*—and whom no one seems to have been prepared for. The combination has proven irresistible—to fans, to the sportscasters and sportswriters, to folks who'd never thought they were interested in the game—making Ichiro-mania something that few can stop talking about.

For all the attention from America's media and the adulation of Seattle's body-painted, headband-wearing fans, Ichiro has said his highest honor is to fit in and be accepted as a part of this no-less-than remarkable Mariners team. He does fit in, in a way only he might have predicted.

When the BlueWave won the Japan Series in 1996, Ichiro derided their opponent as a team of gaudy stars—"a team without craftsmen."

Ichiro has reached out to our yearning for something more artistic, more beautiful to behold, than just another going-going-gone.

Doesn't seem entirely gracious, but Ichiro's point was this: Not only had the other side not mastered the details of the game, they did not play together as a team.

In other words, more stale thinking: The ultimate expression of the craft of baseball is the building of a powerful team. By that measure, the Mariners look pretty good.

THE BEST IS YET TO COME

Roger Hansen, a former coach for the Mariners who now works with Orix's catchers, has watched Ichiro for two years. Although many of Ichiro's hits in the majors have been legged-out choppers in the infield,

Hansen believes Ichiro's just getting started. "I'm sure he wanted to establish himself over there."

Where was Ichiro trying to establish himself? On the inside part of the plate. As Ichiro has said: "If you can't hit fastballs inside, you get a label stuck on you and pitchers will bust you inside forever."

Racking up large numbers of infield hits, the way he did his first few years as a regular in Japan, would not seem to be Ichiro's goal, Hansen contends. The infield hits he's gotten are because of the pitches he's seen—a lot of change-ups outside—pitches he can put in play and beat out for singles while still taking care of business inside.

When Ichiro burst on the Japanese scene, infield hits accounted for nearly a sixth of his 210 hits. They became his trademark. But that changed. In his next season, he finished three home runs shy of winning the triple crown. His consolation prize was to be the league's top base stealer, going 49-for-58.

Isao Ojimi, a scout for the New York Mets and once the only person in the world who thought Mets outfielder Tsuyoshi Shinjo was major league material, expected Ichiro to hit over .300, with 50 stolen bases, and "if he tries, 20 home runs. He might not hit for as high an average though."

Yet, Ichiro's two hitting streaks of 22 and 23 consecutive games, his first-half batting average of .347, his league-leading number of hits,

The ultimate expression of the craft of baseball is the building of a powerful team. By that measure, the Mariners look pretty good.

steals, and runs, and his being a key member of a team with the second-best record ever before the All-Star break have left few non-believers. Even Hansen, who is used to seeing magic from the Wizard, was stunned: "Of course, we thought he'd be good, but to go over there and just start ripping it up over there the way he has. No one predicted that."

Mariners manager Piniella puts it matter-of-factly: "Ichiro has answered every call. He's answered every question . . . He's a full package."

At the All-Star Game, Minnesota Twins shortstop Cristian Guzman, regarded by many as the fastest in the game, tipped his hat to Ichiro, whose dash to first has been timed at 3.7 seconds. "He may be faster than me. He's the man now."

But if Ichiro's the man now, what's left?

A lot, says Hansen. "He's done great. They've seen his fielding and his arm and his speed, but they still haven't seen the whole Ichiro yet. He's got so much more to show them."

Ichiro is the perfect example of the simple truth that those who give their all, find even more to give.

And we are happy to receive.

JIM ALLEN is the baseball columnist for the English-language *Daily Yomiuri* and has been researching Japanese baseball since he landed in Japan in 1984. He first stumbled across the name of Ichiro Suzuki while examining minor league performances following the 1992 season.

STATISTICS

Ichiro's Statistics in Japan's Pacific League

Year	G	AB	R	H	2B	3B	HR
1992	40	95	9	24	5	0	0
1993	43	64	4	12	2	0	1
1994	130	546*	111*	210*	41*	5	13
1995	130	524	104*	179*	23	4	25
1996	130	542*	104*	193*	24	4	16
1997	135	536	94*	185*	31	4	17
1998	135	506	79	181*	36	3	13
1999	103	411	80	141	27	2	21
2000	105	395	73	153	22	1	12
JAPAN TOTAL	951	3619	658	1278	211	23	118

Ichiro's Statistics in the American League (through August 15, 2001)

Year	G	AB	R	H	2B	3B	HR
2001	117	524	98*	178*	29	8	6

* = league leader
+ = second place
IBB = intentional base on balls
CS = caught stealing

RBI	BB	IBB	SO	SB	CS	OBP	SLG	AVG
5	3	0	11	3	2	.276	.305	.253
3	2	0	7	0	2	.212	.266	.188
54	51	8	53	29	7	.445*	.549	.385*
80*	68	17*	52	49*	9	.432*	.544	.342*
84	56	13*	57	35	3	.422*	.504	.356*
91	62	14*	36	39	4	.414	.513	.345*
71	43	15*	35	11	4	.414	.518	.358*
68	45	15*	46	12	1	.412*	.572	.343*
73	54	16*	36	21	1	.460*	.539	.387*
529	384	98	333	199	33	.421	.522	.353
60	23	7	36	40+	10	.373	.460	.340

HONORS AND AWARDS

1992
· Batting title (.366 average),
      Western League
· MVP, Minor League All-Star Game

1994
· Batting title (.385 average),
      Pacific League
· New record: 210 hits in 130 games
· Golden Glove Award
· MVP, Pacific League

1995
· Batting title (.342 average),
      Pacific League
· Most Stolen Bases
· Golden Glove Award
· MVP, Pacific League

1996
· Batting title (.356 average),
      Pacific League
· Golden Glove Award
· MVP, Pacific League

1997
· Batting title (.345 average),
      Pacific League
· Golden Glove Award

1998
· Batting title (.358 average),
      Pacific League
· Golden Glove Award

1999
· Batting title (.343 average),
      Pacific League
· Golden Glove Award

2000
· Batting title (.387 average),
      Pacific League
· Golden Glove Award

IN THE UNITED STATES

2001
· All-Star Game, Most Votes Received,
      American League
· All-Star Game, Most Votes Received,
      Major Leagues

NOTES

The following references provided extra source material in the writing of the commentary:

Finnegan, Bob, "Expect Mariners to Bid for Japanese Outfielder Suzuki," *Seattle Times,* October 31, 2000.

Grant, Evan, "Ichiro's Homer Spoils Rangers' Rally," *Dallas Morning News,* July 3, 2001.
> Quote from Ivan "Pudge" Rodriguez: "Right now, Ichiro is the best player in baseball. . . ."

Haudricourt, Tom, "Ichiro Energizes All-Star Selections," *Milwaukee Journal Sentinel,* July 3, 2001.
> Quote from Ichiro Suzuki: "I did not expect or imagine that I would be a starter . . ."

Komatsu, Narumi, *Ichiro Intabyu* (The Ichiro interview): *Attack the Pinnacle!* Tokyo: Shinchosha, 2001.
> Quotes from Ichiro Suzuki:
> "It made me so happy . . ." (Komatsu, p. 113);
> "It was all about what I needed to learn . . ." (Komatsu, p. 118);
> "More than junior high school, more than high school. . . ." (Komatsu, p. 118);
> "I was watching him and didn't think he was spectacularly good. . . ." (Komatsu, p. 120);

"I was thinking, 'What if there was a different coach every
        year? . . .'" (Komatsu, p. 129);

"Kawamura quickly recognized my peculiar characteristics . . ."
        (Komatsu, p. 129);

"I think there are different kinds of championships."
        (Komatsu, p. 138);

"The pitches Irabu threw in that game . . ." (Komatsu, p. 136);

"Winning is the most important thing. . . ." (Komatsu, p. 142);

Regarding Akira Ogi: "I guess it would be all right for you . . ."
        (Komatsu, p. 89);

Regarding Nobuyuki Suzuki: "Life comes but once . . ."
        (Komatsu, p. 93);

"If I'm going to surprise American fans . . . " (Komatsu, p. 83);

"If you can't hit fastballs inside . . ." (Komatsu, p. 29).

Puronogenfukei (Portrait of a professional's origins). Baseball Album No. 119.
Tokyo: Baseball Magazine Sha, 2001.
> Quote from Go Nakamura: "He was something else when it came
> to his power of concentration . . ."

Sherwin, Bob, "Ichiro Takes First At-bat in Stride," *Seattle Times,* July 11, 2001.
> Quote from Cristian Guzman: "He may be faster than me . . .";
> Quote from Ichiro Suzuki: "First of all, I'm very honored to face
> Randy . . ."

Suda, Juri, "Junior All-Star MVP Interview," *Shukan Baseball Magazine*, August
31, 1992.

Suzuki, Nobuyuki, *Chichi to musuko: Ichiro to watashi no 21 nen* (Father and son: My
21 Years with Ichiro). Tokyo: Futami Shobo, 1995.

Thiel, Art, "No Angst in All-Star Ichiro," *Seattle Post-Intelligencer*, July 6, 2001.

    Quote from Ichiro Suzuki: "I'm just setting them up . . .";

    Quote from Lou Piniella: "Ichiro has answered every call . . ."

Anecdote about Don Nomura and Mac Suzuki, from Robert Whiting, author, from his interview with Don Nomura, Tokyo, April 1999.

Anecdote about Ichiro, his car, and the press, from Midori Wakabayashi, reporter, *Daily Sports*, telephone conversation, July 5, 2001.

Author's interviews:

    Roger Hansen, Tokyo, July 2, 2001;

    Isao Ojimi, telephone interview, July 4, 2001;

    So Taguchi, Tokyo, July 2, 2001.

Quote about Ichiro Suzuki as "the new face of Japan," from *Newsweek*, July 15, 1996.

Statement from Mike Hargrove on Ichiro Suzuki's ability to play in the major leagues, from Hargrove's speaking to reporters at Tokyo Dome, November 1998.

Cover design by Bradford Foltz
Book design by Fritz Metsch
Produced and edited by Elmer Luke

Front cover photograph © 2001 Robert Beck/MLB Photos
Back cover photograph © 2001 Bill Sallaz/MLB Photos
Frontispiece photograph by Brad Mangin/Sports Illustrated

Printed in the United States of America
by Color Art, St. Louis, Missouri,
under supervision by Toppan Printing Co., Ltd.

www.thejapanpage.com

KODANSHA INTERNATIONAL LTD.